NEXT STOP:
ST.LOUIS UNION STATION

NEXT STOP:

S T .   L O U I S

UNION STATION

Edward C. Parker

The Patrice Press
St. Louis, Missouri

Library of Congress
Cataloging-In-Publication Data

The Patrice Press
1701 S. Eighth Street
St. Louis MO 63104

Printed in the United States of America

To the grandfather I never knew, Jesse Everingham, and to my uncles, Arthur Everingham, Charles Everingham, and Ernest Carr, all Terminal Railroad men; and to my grandmother, Myrtle Uplinger Everingham, who raised her young family alone; and finally to the wonderful young woman whose support and encouragement kept this dream alive—my wife, Debbie.

Preface and Acknowledgments

The purpose of this publication is to share some old photographs from the early days of Union station. The book is presented in two parts: the first is a brief history of the construction and grand opening; the second consists of reproductions of original illustrations of the station.

Next Stop: St. Louis Union Station is the result of good fortune and research. Good fortune in finding the old photographs and research materials in the collections at the State Historical Society of Missouri, in Ellis Library at the University of Missouri in Columbia, and in the St. Louis Public Library.

Most of the photographs were taken around 1894. They first appeared in the Terminal Railroad Association's *The St. Louis Union Station, A Monograph.* Other valuable sources of information include Norbury Wayman's fine history, *St. Louis Union Station and Its Railroads;* the Terminal Railroad Association's *Report of Chief Engineer . . . 1902-04;* M. Patricia

Holmes's article "The St. Louis Union Station" from the Missouri Historical Society's *Bulletin;* and of particular value, the St. Louis *Globe-Democrat* and *Post-Dispatch* of September 1 and 2, 1894, describing the opening of the station.

I wish to express my gratitude to Missouri University's Ellis Library and to my friends and colleagues at the State Historical Society of Missouri in Columbia for their help and encouragement. Special mentions go to Leona Morris for trying to help me overcome that bane of all writers—the "was" and "were" words; to Peggy Platner for her unabashed enthusiasm for the pictures; to Doug Hurt and Kathy Dains for their advice regarding book publishing; to Professor Sid Larson, art gallery curator, whose early appraisal of the project, "It's a natural," was a definite spur; to Ara Kaye for her competent assistance in the newspaper library; to former employee Sue Yeshilada for reading the manuscript; and to my co-workers in the reference library, Laurel Boeckman and Liz Bailey, for putting up with me during the project.

Additional appreciation is due Orval Henderson, Missouri Department of Natural Resources, who provided early expertise and kept this project alive. Jeff Mills of the Patrice Press staff worked long hours clarifying the captions.

And finally, to my other reader, Debbie Parker, a special thank you and a cup of hot chocolate.

Edward C. Parker
February 24, 1989

UNION STATION

Welcome to St. Louis Union Station. This triumph of architectural grandeur opened with great fanfare in 1894 and served the city's rail passengers for more than eighty years. During its peak years, Union Station handled 100,000 passengers a day and managed over 240 train movements each an hour. (By comparison, at Lambert-St. Louis International Airport, the sixth busiest airport in the nation, about 80 planes take off and land each hour and approximately 55,000 passengers arrive or depart per day.)

During the 1904 World's Fair, one train left the station every minute, taking visitors to that extravaganza. Thousands of European immigrants came through the station on their way to a new life. In the 1920s Queen Marie of Rumania, darling of international society, arrived at Union Station in her luxurious private railroad car. William Jennings Bryan, the golden tongued orator and perennial presidential candidate, walked through its concourses. So did Theodore Roosevelt, Franklin Roosevelt, Jack Dempsey, Bill "Bojangles" Robinson, and Will Rogers.

In 1942 thousands of jubilant St. Louisans met their World Champion Cardinals at Union Station when they returned from defeating the New York Yankees. Poet T. S. Eliot left from its platform on his way to Harvard. Fannie Hurst took a train from Union Station to New York and fame as one of the most successful writers of all time.

For fifty years campaigning politicians made it a regular stop on their itineraries. It was from the rear platform of a train at Union Station in 1948 that newly elected President Harry S. Truman triumphantly flourished the *Chicago Tribune's* headline: "Dewey Defeats Truman." British Prime Minister Winston Churchill stopped at the station on his way to Fulton, Missouri, where he delivered his historic "Iron Curtain" speech.

For almost seventy-five years the station's Fred Harvey Restaurant was a favorite meeting place for special birthdays, holidays, and after-the-prom gatherings. At the station's private dining room, dignitaries dined in an intimate and elegant atmosphere.

One hundred and fifty redcaps kept baggage moving smoothly, and dozens of vendors, barbers, shoeshine boys, and pants-pressers kept passengers happy. In the station's early years bathtubs were available for the use of ladies, and bathinettes were provided for infants.

During the two world wars the station was packed with soldiers itching to get to the front—and then just as eager to get back home. Thousands of sweethearts, wives, and mothers stood by the gates, waiting. . . . And hundreds of flag-draped coffins were delivered to Union Station.

Some of America's favorite trains used the station: Missouri Pacific's Sunshine Special and Pacific Eagle (also known as the Kirkwood Eagle, since it doubled as a commuter line); The Wabash Banner Blue and Cannonball; the Illinois Central's Green Diamond; the Frisco's Texas Special and Meteor; and the Gulf, Mississippi & Ohio's Ann Rutledge.

Following World War II the rapid growth of air travel led to a dramatic decline in railroad passenger service, and the station fell into a long period of neglect and gradual decay.

In 1978 Amtrak transferred its remaining passenger trains to a nearby temporary station. At the same time, the mortgage was forclosed. It looked as if the venerable station were doomed.

Fortunately, a bankruptcy petition filed at the last minute halted a threatened foreclosure auction, which probably would have meant the razing of the station. A group of St. Louis businessmen formed the St. Louis Station Associates and began the long process of saving one of the city's best-known landmarks.

A buyer was found—Oppenheimer Properties of New York—which recognized the potential in the station. Oppenheimer hired the Rouse Company of Columbia, Maryland, to begin restoration. Working with the local architectural firm of Hellmuth, Obata, and Kassabaum, Rouse developers insisted on authentic restoration. Meticulous research was done to determine exactly how the station looked when it formally opened on September 1, 1894.

The result, celebrated with pageantry in the second grand opening held August 29, 1985, is a magnificent recreation of an opulent era now long gone. The architectural and decorative details of the station can be appreciated anew.

The original cost of building the station in the 1890s was $6.5 million. The 1979 purchase price was $5 million. The cost of the five-year restoration was $150 million, at that time the most expensive restoration project in the nation.

Today St. Louis Union Station hums with a different kind of activity than the smoking, chuffing locomotives of its early years. Still, there are thousands of travelers who visit it: sightseers who want to experience the past in the present, shoppers looking for unique gifts, diners seeking meals in a special atmosphere. These people are not very different from those who visited the station in the 1890s. They marvel at its elegance and enjoy its beauty.

THE GATEWAY

In 1874, with the opening of that engineering wonder, Eads Bridge, St. Louis rapidly developed into a major railroad center. The great barrier of the Mississippi River had been spanned; no longer did trains running east and west bypass the Gateway City. St. Louis welcomed the chance to grow.

The city's first passenger station, Union Depot, was built at Twelfth and Poplar streets in 1875. During the next two decades the city doubled its population and its commercial importance. Union Depot was quickly outgrown.

As rail traffic increased, so did the number of railroads serving the city. In 1889 a consortium of six rail lines was formed, calling itself the Terminal Railroad Association of St. Louis (TRRA). Its aim was to enlarge the city's terminal facilities, both for passengers and for freight, and to consolidate the scattered railyards.

The foremost goal was to build a new passenger station, one that would be the largest, most elegant, and most comfortable in America—and maybe in the world. Dr. William Taussig, president of the Terminal Railroad Association, was the driving force behind the dream and kept it alive for five years.

The first step was to locate a site. The new station should be situated about midway between the north and south extremes of the city. That placed it about one and one-fourth miles west of the Mississippi River and about five miles east of the city limits.

Streetcar lines from all parts of the city should be able to reach the station easily. The business district and downtown hotels should be within walking distance.

All these "shoulds" met in one spot—the six city blocks between Clark Avenue and Market Street, Eighteenth and Twentieth Streets.

But the forty-two-acre site was already covered with streets, houses, and commercial buildings. In that area stood one of the largest flour mills and its warehouses, the stables and car shed of a major streetcar line, a gas company plant, a wagon factory, about eighty multi-story brick houses, and one of the largest breweries in St. Louis, occupying almost one square block. South of Clark Avenue, where the train yard's powerhouse was eventually built, were a soap and candle factory, several rows of residences, great coal sheds, and more warehouses.

All these buildings had to be leveled. An ordinance enacted in 1891 allowed owners to be compensated for their property and demolition began in February 1892.

Because of the area's topography, railroad approaches to St. Louis were most practical through the narrow Mill Creek Valley, which paralleled Market Street. The relatively flat terrain in the area of old Chouteau's Pond at Twentieth Street, which had been filled in after the cholera epidemic of 1849, looked like a promising area for a railyard.

Once the site was chosen for the new station, the architectural design had to be determined. The TRRA board of directors adopted an "end station" plan because no through trains were to run beyond the city from east or west. Passengers continuing past St. Louis transferred to other lines.

This meant that all railway lines, thirteen from the east and nine from the west, would converge and pour out their passengers at one point. A large depot was needed, one that could accommodate restaurants, retail shops, a hotel, and other services.

The TRRA initiated a competition in March 1891 to find the right architect for the new station. Ten architects from throughout the United States were invited to submit drawings. Eight of them did. On July 1, 1891, Theodore C. Link of St. Louis was awarded "First Premium" of $10,000 for the best design.

Born in Germany in 1850, Link was educated in Europe. In 1870 he came to the United States, and by 1873 he was employed by the Atlantic & Pacific Railroad in St. Louis. After working as assistant chief engineer at Forest Park, he became superintendent of the public parks in St. Louis.

Turning to architecture in the 1880s, Link was influenced by the great H. H. Richardson, who was known for his enthusiasm for ''Romanesque bulk''—large arches and massive limestone blocks. Link's work includes the Alton Public Library, St. Mark's Episcopal Church, and the Wabash Railroad's Vandeventer Station. Link also served as consulting engineer for St. Louis City Hall. Later he designed the Mississippi state capitol and buildings on the Louisiana State University campus. His major achievement was St. Louis Union Station.

Link began work as soon as he was informed of his commission to design the station. His subsequent appointment as superintendent of construction gave him complete control of building the headhouse, the main building in the complex.

After his plans were accepted, Link began to study travelers. Every day for six months he went to the old Union Depot to watch passengers coming and going. He talked with them and learned of their wants and needs. He then modeled the new station in accordance with the ideas he developed.

DESIGN AND CONSTRUCTION

Link's original plans called for a building more than 450 feet long. During construction the property adjacent to the building on the west was obtained, adding 150 feet to the tract and requiring a revision of the western end of the building. Although the finished structure differed from the original design in length, the floor plan remained essentially unchanged. The additional 12,000 square feet became the Terminal Hotel and retail shops.

Preparing the foundation in April presented a number of problems. As the TRRA's publication stated,

> On the eastern portion [of the site] the ground was undermined for some considerable distance with a network of caves and vaults, the interesting remains of the oldest brewery in the city. These subterraneous passages were below the sewer system, and filled with water immediately after being exposed.

The ground encountered in the center of the building site proved excellent, but

> . . . the western end led us directly into an arm of the historic Chouteau Pond, where willow stumps, log cabins and the hulls of primitive boats were encountered twenty feet below the surface. This region was formerly famous for its springs, and an inconvenient number of them caused much vexatious delay by their sudden appearance.

Concrete footings were used for the most part. No wooden piles were used to support the head-house. The foundation for the clock tower was entirely disconnected from the rest of the foundation. Slip joints were used between the tower and the abutting walls, allowing for a settlement of one-half inch. The foundation walls terminated in a granite base at the grade line.

After more than a year of demolition and excavation, the foundation work was completed. With the end of that phase of construction came the placing of the cornerstone on July 8, 1893.

During the next thirteen months and twenty-four days, the great building arose under the watchful eyes of architect Link and general contractor J. Willard Adams, a well-known St. Louis builder.

Link selected a Romanesque style for the station because its heaviness expressed well the character and purpose of the structure. It was "a modern elaboration of the feudal gateway," serving as the means of entrance and exit to a city, much like the bastioned gates of medieval times.

The headhouse along Market Street included the massive east pavilion, where the clock tower rose; the central pavilion flanked by round towers; and the hotel complex, which was not completed until 1895. South of the headhouse, stretching the length of the building from east to west in a narrow corridor fifty feet wide, was the midway, which separated the headhouse from the massive train shed.

The train shed, designed by George H. Pegram, originally measured 606' x 630' with a roof height of 98 feet at the center. Work on the foundations began in April 1892, and the structure was ready for use by November 1893. More than 2,700 tons of steel, 95,000 square feet of glass, and 961,000 board feet of lumber were used in its construction. Three and one-half miles of track were laid.

Inside and outside the building, Link and Louis Millet, the interior decorator, mixed and matched the most elegant styles of the day. The west wing was Gothic, the Grand Hall rather Moorish, the dining room Viennese. Marble from Belgium, Africa, Georgia, Tennessee, Vermont, and New York was used.

The architectural detail was admired and criticized, talked and written about for years. No one came away from the Union Station unimpressed.

The Grand Opening

The forecast for September 1, 1894, read "generally fair today with stationary temperatures." Actually, temperatures pushed into the nineties in the afternoon, and by evening the weather was still pleasantly warm.

A crowd began arriving early at the new Union Station for its scheduled 7:30 P.M. opening. Fourteen thousand printed invitations had been sent and each holder was permitted to bring as many ladies as he wanted, but no children were allowed. The daily St. Louis newspapers declared that the new station would draw the wealthiest and most fashionable people in St. Louis for its dedication ceremonies. Indeed, some 20,000 came.

As the carriages wound their way to the crowded Market Street entrance, the impressive structure came into view. It was the largest station in the world, larger than the renowned Union Depot of Frankfurt, Germany, or Reading Station of Philadelphia.

The carriages arrived via well-publicized routes. For instance, those arriving from the north and west approached on Pine and Chestnut streets, went south on Twentieth to Market, and then east to the main entrance.

Despite the majesty of Union Station, it was almost impossible not to notice the unsightly buildings across Market Street. The row of squalid shops, chiefly ticket scalpers, cheap restaurants and saloons, detracted from the station's imposing facade. At least one journalist of the time called for the widening of Market Street and the creation of a park, modeled after similar parks at European railway stations. It was believed that such a park would "bring the structure into the prominence that its architectural beauty demands."

That took some time. Almost fifty years later Aloe Plaza, with its remarkable Milles fountain, was dedicated. In the 1960s the rest of the ramshackle buildings on Market Street were cleared.

Those entering the station on its opening night found the structure brilliantly illuminated from basement to attic. Flowers and potted plants lined the waiting rooms, arcades, galleries, and corridors. The crowd wandered through the station, marveling at its architecture and praising Taussig and Link.

The evening was planned as an informal affair, although some visitors wore evening clothes. Guests refreshed themselves at the restaurant and lunch counters. Music—primarily waltzes and

OPENING NIGHT

On September 1, 1894, St. Louis Union Station opened. Some of the 20,000 persons who attended the celebration are pictured here in the Grand Hall.

marches—was provided by Guido B. Vogel's two military bands and two orchestras, which played at various locations in the station.

After the crowds explored the building from headhouse to train shed, they assembled in the midway to listen to speeches. The speakers included, among others, Taussig, St. Louis Mayor Cyrus P. Walbridge, and the former governor of Missouri, David R. Francis. (Francis would gain world renown as president of the St. Louis World's Fair in 1904.)

Taussig appeared elated as he bowed to the chairman who had introduced him and turned to the great crowd surrounding the speaker's stand. He described what the railroads hoped to accomplish in terms of passenger comfort. Then he pointed out some of the more important features of the station, sketching the various departments. He praised highly the Terminal Railroad Association and Theodore Link.

Other speakers also praised the station and the men responsible for it. By the time the echoes of the last speaker had died, great tribute had been paid. As the visiting throng dispersed from the building, the station remained open to fulfill its purpose. The first train to arrive at the new facility was the Vandalia fast mail from New York, at 1:45 A.M. At 2:30 A.M. the Burlington fast mail departed over the St. Louis, Keokuk & Northwestern line. The Missouri Pacific fast mail left for the West at 3 A.M. And the first passenger train out of the station, the

St. Louis, Kansas City & Colorado, or Creve Coeur Lake train, left at 5:50 A.M.

Today it is almost impossible to appreciate the impact and importance of the railroads in the United States between 1850 and 1950. At the turn of the century one-fifth of the population of almost 70 million derived a living from occupations connected with the railways.

Although railroad passenger traffic has dwindled, freight traffic has grown, and the St. Louis metropolitan area today is the third largest rail center in the nation.

The day of the opulent railroad station is over. Yet its memory lingers in the magnificent restoration of Union Station. Most of the photographs that follow were taken by B. A. Atwater of Chicago, shortly before the grand opening. They can be compared with the present-day renovation, allowing visitors to imagine the resplendence of the station's early years. There was nothing like it, and there never will be again.

UNION STATION
1894

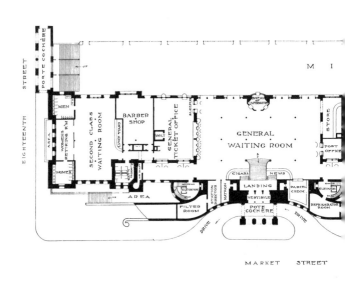

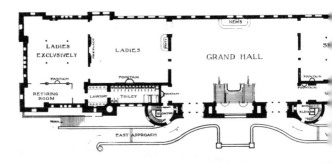

Orginal Floor Plan of Union Station

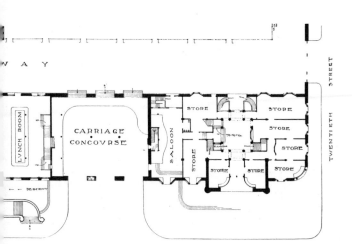

LVNCH ROOM

CARRIAGE
CONCOVRSE

STORE STORE

STORE

TO HOTEL STORE

STORE

STORE STORE STORE

SALOON

STORE

DESCENT

W A Y

TWENTIETH STREET

CAFE DINING HALL

SERVING ROOM

KITCHEN

GVESTS CHAMBERS

CORRIDOR

LIGHT SHAFT

HOTEL PARLOR

CORRIDOR

GVESTS CHAMBERS

LOBBY

TOILET

CORRIDOR

ROTVNDA

CORRIDOR

PRIVATE DINING ROOM

GVESTS CHAMBERS

OFFICE

CORRIDOR

GVESTS CHAMBERS

RIDOR

GVESTS CHAMBERS

UNION STATION

This India ink line drawing was submitted by winning architect Theodore C. Link of St. Louis as part of his original entry in the competition. The two main fronts are shown in plane perspective at the corner of Eighteenth and Market streets. The drawing, which was executed on a scale of one-eighth inch to the foot, measured over six feet wide. The towers at right rear were not included in the final plan.

VIEW FROM NINETEENTH STREET

This view from Nineteenth Street shows the headhouse almost completed. During construction the property directly to the west was purchased and incorporated into the plans. This addition increased the length of the headhouse from 455′9″ to 606′, but did not greatly alter the floor plan. The extra space was alloted to the Terminal Hotel and stores in the west end of the structure. The hotel was the only feature of St. Louis Union Station not completed by the opening on September 1, 1894. It began operation the following year.

CARRIAGE CONCOURSE

Just opposite Nineteenth Street, west of the station's main entrance, are three large archways. Through these, vehicles passed into the carriage concourse. Shown here facing north toward the Market Street exits, the concourse separated the station from the hotel annex.

MARKET STREET PORTE COCHERE

The main entrance on Market Street featured this beautifully worked porte cochere. Passengers could step out of their horse-drawn coaches beneath its protection and pass through the doors onto the landing of the grand staircase. From there they could ascend to the Grand Hall or descend to the general waiting room. The porte cochere was removed when Market Street was widened in 1911.

MAIN ENTRANCE

Spacious terraced walkways from east and west led to the station's main entrances, two wide arched doorways. They were situated above the ground floor entrance and flanked an arched stained glass window. The western walkway, pictured here, is 16′ x 50′. From Market Street it rises gracefully with sweeping curves, which were designed to lessen the labor of climbing by pleasing the eye. Before its removal in 1911 the balcony atop the porte cochere commanded an excellent view of the thoroughfare.

ELECTROLIER

Ornamental iron and bronze fixtures holding arc lights, called electroliers, were situated on massive pillars along the two approaches to the main entrance. They represented the braziers that were hung before feudal castles to welcome guests. Union Station was one of the first buildings in the city to be lit entirely with electricity. Some of the station's 3,600 original handmade bulbs are still functional today.

EAST APPROACH

This scene of strollers on the eastern walkway portrays the fortress-like grandeur envisioned by the architect. The round tower contains stairs to the office floors above the station, as well as an elevator for passengers with special needs. The twin tower farther west is similarly equipped. The narrow windows are reminiscent of the arrow slits used to defend medieval European castles.

SUSPENDEND CEILING

St. Louis Union Station is an example of the application of practical Victorian inventiveness to lofty artistic aspirations. This photograph, taken during construction, shows the many cables and girders used to support the immense vaulted ceiling of the Grand Hall.

EAST PAVILION

Looking east down the walkway from the main entrances, an impressive array of stone- and metal-work is visible. It has stood the test of time, both artistically and structurally. The base of the clock tower is slightly to the left of center. The clock tower sits on an entirely separate foundation. Slip joints were used between the tower and the abutting walls.

CLOCK TOWER

The clock tower, built on the highest point of the site, rises 230 feet above the old track level. The four clock dials each measure ten feet in diameter. The tower also served as the intake for fresh air, which was forced by fans into the heating system and then through ceiling vents into various rooms.

EAST PAVILION

Arched windows, at projections along the front facade, were intentionally subdued, but were not overpowered by the magnificence of the structure. This window on the east pavilion faces north.

41

PORTE COCHERE

The Eighteenth Street exit was designed to be the station's primary exit. This elaborate porte cochere, which extended over a driveway adjacent to the street, provided passengers with relative shelter from the elements as they boarded horse-drawn conveyances. Like the Market and Eighteenth street facades, it is faced with Bedford (Indiana) limestone.

Midway

This view through the ornamental wrought iron gates of one of the three arches of the Eighteenth Street exit shows the full length of the midway. The gates to the platforms are on the left; the rear of the headhouse is on the right. The midway measured 606' x 50'. Its floor was granitoid and the roof, two stories above, was glass and iron, with light steel trusses. The south side (left) was originally open to the tracks, exposing travelers to the heat or cold of the season.

AVENUE OF BUMPERS

As many as thirty trains could be accommodated at one time along these platforms under the station's huge shed. The thirty tracks had a combined length of three and one-half miles. (Later, twelve more tracks were added.) Ornate iron fences separated the platforms from the midway. Large safety bumpers (bearing track numbers) prevented trains from overrunning the midway. The stationmaster's office is at upper right, and the 300-foot long baggage house is in the background.

STATIONMASTER'S OFFICE

This kiosk was centrally located against the midway fence facing tracks 15 and 16. Inside was a bulletin board announcing arriving trains, an office where conductors received instructions telegraphed from the switch tower, and the stationmaster's office. The stationmaster was responsible for virtually everything in the train shed: the movement of trains, the activities of employees, and the enforcement of rules. All gatemen, gate police, platform porters, and messengers reported directly to the stationmaster.

SECONDARY EXIT

The secondary exit, at the west end of the mid-way, is an arch thirty-six feet wide which leads to Twentieth Street. Directly to the left (south) was the baggage house. To the right, in the rear of the headhouse, were entrances to the hotel and a variety of shops.

THE MIDWAY

Even at midnight the midway was full of travelers. This view looks east, toward the Eighteenth Street exit.

GENERAL WAITING ROOM

The general waiting room, just off the midway, measured 76′ x 120′ and provided spacious comfort for travelers awaiting their trains. Along the four walls of this room were ticket windows, a telegraph office, public telephones, a post office, a checkroom for parcels, a "bureau of information" ready to answer questions, and vendors selling fruit, candy, and cigars. Short corridors led from the waiting room to a barbershop, lavatories, and a lunchroom. The eighteen-foot high ceiling was supported by twelve beautiful scagliola marble columns. The grand staircase was on the north wall.

GRAND STAIRCASE

The grand staircase connects the general waiting room with the Grand Hall above. The landing, halfway between floors, is at the level of the street outside. Doors led from the landing to the covered Market Street entrance.

ALLEGORY WINDOW

This stained glass window, designed by Theodore Link, portrays St. Louis between fair San Francisco and the more somber New York. The trees behind San Francisco bear oranges and lemons, while those behind New York bear apples and peaches. St. Louis holds a sheaf of grain. Behind her rises the Old Courthouse.

The allegory represents the importance of St. Louis as a connection between the two coasts. The window, executed by the St. Louis firm of W. W. Davis and George W. Chambers, is located on the north wall of the Grand Hall, above the grand staircase and the Market Street entrance.

WHISPERING ARCH

The gold arch over the Market Street entrance, forty feet wide, makes an elaborate frame for the beautiful glass window. It is known as the "whispering arch" because when two people stand at opposite ends of the arch and whisper, they can hear each other clearly.

GRAND HALL

The immense Grand Hall, shown here from the west, was designed to be the pièce de résistance of the station. It measures 70'x 120'. Its barrel-vaulted ceiling rises sixty-five feet above the interlocking English floor tile. Dark green ceramic tile decorates the base of the walls. Above is light green scagliola marble with yellow veining. The eighteen-foot walls are capped by a frieze detailed in gold. Above this, on the east and west walls, magnificent low-relief traceries radiate over forty-foot wide arches. The figures of seven women bearing stained glass torches emerge from each of the traceries. The relief work was sculpted so that dust accumulations would enchance the design by intensifying the lines.

The north wall features the grand staircase and the "whispering arch" with its stained glass window. To either side of the stair are the main en-

trances coming from the walkways above Market
Street. The second and third stories of the north
wall are intricately detailed arcaded galleries.
The ceiling panels are yellow-green with sten-
ciling, and the ornamental ribs between them
are covered with gold.

The wrought iron ''electrolier'' suspended
from the ceiling was twenty feet in diameter,
weighed over two tons, and held 350 lights. It
was removed for scrap during World War II.

GRAND HALL ARCADE

Beyond the huge arches at the east and west ends of the Grand Hall, on the second floor, are recessed arcades. The western arcade, pictured here, is a fine example of the elaborate detail used even in areas which did not receive heavy use. The background of these arcades and of the galleries on the north wall were done in muted blue to give the illusion of immense depth.

DRINKING FOUNTAIN

This drinking fountain was set in a recess at the north end of the Grand Hall's eastern wall, near the eastern elevator. It was made of Sienna marble and featured a Venetian glass mosaic which depicted a water nymph.

LADIES WAITING ROOM

This double archway led east from the Grand Hall to the wing set aside for women travelers. The first room, visible through the arches, was a spacious sitting room for the use of ladies in the company of gentlemen. Beyond it was another room exclusively for women, with access to lavatories and a screened off "retiring room" with lounges.

All of these areas and their attendants were supervised by a matron representing the Women's Aid Society, which saw to the needs of women traveling alone.

FIREPLACE

The focal point of the waiting room for ladies traveling with gentlemen was this elaborate fireplace. The mantel was constructed of Numidian marble. In the plaster niche above stood the life-size statue of a young woman holding aloft a clock dial.

WAITING ROOM

The waiting room for ladies with gentlemen is shown here from another entrance just south of the main double archway. For this room a color scheme of cream, light pink, and delicate blue was chosen. Enameled German tile was used for the wainscoting and Belgian tile was used in the floor mosaic.

The room contained a fireplace and a drinking fountain, as well as fruit stand not visible in this picture. The intricate stencil details here and elsewhere sometimes required ten or more colors to achieve the desired effect.

73

LADIES WAITING ROOM

This waiting room was for the use of women only. Oak wainscoting and a frieze of roses were chosen to give the room a homelike air. The northern section of the room, visible at right, was partitioned off as a retiring room where ill or weary women travelers could rest in privacy on lounges. West of the retiring room was a doorway leading to the women's bathing facilities.

VIEW FROM WAITING ROOM

This view looks west through a series of rooms from the waiting room for ladies. Through the first archway is the sitting room for ladies accompanied by gentlemen. Beyond the second arch is the south side of the Grand Hall. Past the third arch is the gentlemen's smoking room. Beyond that, the open doors to the dining hall are visible.

WEST END OF GRAND HALL

The west end of the Grand Hall is symmetrical to the east end, with the same lofty spaces and complex detail work. The south arch at left and the central double archway lead to the gentlemen's smoking room and to a small cafe beyond. Spittoons were kept within easy reach of the seats between the arches. The north arch, at right, leads to the gothic corridor, through which travelers passed to the dining rooms.

GOTHIC CORRIDOR

This eighty-foot-long passageway, which connects the Grand Hall with the dining hall to the
west, was designed in Tudor-Gothic style. The
elaborate fan-panel ceiling features a row of ornate electric light fixtures that hang like stalac-
tites from the ceiling. The green marble for the
walls came from the Swiss Alps. The arch on the
left leads to the smoking room.

DINING HALL DOORWAY

The doorway to the general dining hall featured stained glass and marble tile. Sculptured torch bearers are on either side. The door to the private dining room, which was reserved for the use of important guests, is visible within.

DINING HALL

The dining hall was finished in old oak and black marble, with a paneled wainscoting ten feet high. The ceiling beams were also oak, with plaster panels frescoed to produce a tapestry effect. The floor is English tile.

On the hall's west wall are doors to the serving room, the private dining room, and a lobby connecting to the hotel. On the east wall, shown in this picture, are doorways to the Gothic corridor and to a small cafe, as well as a stairway leading to the lunchroom below.

PRIVATE DINING ROOM

Distinguished visitors took their meals in the private dining room, shown here looking west from the doorway. The room, designed in Italian Renaissance style, was said to be the most elaborately decorated in the station.

PRIVATE DINING ROOM

The private dining room achieved an air of classic refinement through the use of rich relief ornamentation and subdued colors. The trimmings were in cream and gold on a background of robin's egg blue. On the east wall, shown in this picture, was a painting of Ead's Bridge, the engineering marvel of the era.

SMOKING ROOM

In this room, or in the cafe just west, gentlemen could smoke while awaiting their trains. The arch on the left opens onto the Gothic corridor. The others, on the east wall, lead to the Grand Hall. The room's cigar stand is not shown in this view.

LOCOMOTIVE 106

An astonishing number of trains moved in and out of Union Station pulled by locomotives such as this one. Shortly after the station began operation, one account stated that 247 movements of trains and engines occurred during both the morning and evening rush hours. The precise orchestration necessary to regulate this volume of traffic involved 1,600 switches and signals.

Trainyard Looking North

This view, looking north, shows the trainyard layout. In the foreground at left is the powerhouse where all electricity was generated for the many station buildings and grounds. The largest private electric plant existing at that time, it was so well designed that when it was finally shut down in 1976, the eighty-two-year-old backup system automatically activated.

On top of the powerhouse was the switch tower, nerve center of the trainyard. Also visible in this view, at right center, are the freight company offices, including Wells Fargo and American Express.

VIEW FROM SWITCH TOWER

This view from inside the switch tower shows the Y shape of the tracks leading under the shed. Union Station was designed as an end station, with no through tracks. Trains from either direction moved past the station, then backed down the Y and stopped under the shed. This design was necessitated by the terrain and had several advantages. Passengers could detrain directly at the headhouse, while the smoke, dirt, and noise of the engines were kept out of the shed.

SWITCH TOWER

The switch tower controlled the movement of all trains, switches, and signals on tracks within a 1,500-foot radius. Besides commanding an unobstructed view in all directions, the director in charge was provided with telephone and telegraph service, speaking tubes, and other communication equipment. Thirty miniature semaphore instruments indicated which tracks in the shed were occupied and which trains were ready to move. Other instruments showed which approaches were blocked. Three air whistles, controlled from the switch tower and located on the approaches and in the trainyard, quickly alerted trains which were moving at the wrong time.

INTERLOCKING MACHINE

Along the back wall of the switch tower was the interlocking machine. Its 131 levers electrically controlled the compressed air that operated the station's 130 switches and 103 signals. Two separate systems in the machine lessened the danger of issuing conflicting signals. The first was mechanical—the interlocking bars would not move if an incorrect signal were attempted. Secondly, if the levers were positioned incorrectly, rubber insulators prevented the transmission of a signal.

On the wall above the machine was a scale model of the track system where switch and signal changes were electrically reproduced under the watchful eyes of the lever men.

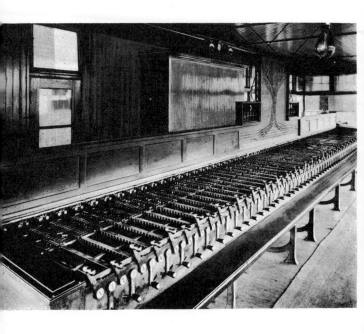

Baggage Handlers

Freight, mail, and baggage cars were kept to the south end of the shed to avoid congestion on the passenger platforms nearer the headhouse.

COMMUNICATIONS CENTER

The fourth floor of the east pavilion was entirely taken up by telephone and telegraph operations.

TRAIN SHED

The construction of Union Station's train shed drew international acclaim as an engineering feat. Over 2,700 tons of steel, 95,000 square feet

of glass, and 961,000 board feet of lumber were used. The shed was designed by George H. Pegram and measured 606′ x 630′ before it was enlarged in 1902. It was and still is the largest single-span train shed in the world.